Healing Words

TO INSPIRE, REMEMBER, AND KNOW

As Told by Source

Penned by Victoria Wright

Illustrations by Jessica Rink

Published February 28, 2021

DISCLAIMER

Illustrations by: Jessica Rink
Book layout by: Karyn Savory, Sweet & Savory Designs

www.HealingWords.online

ISBN: 978-1-7364900-0-6

Foreward

Some call me God. Others call me Source. Still others call me Spirit. I am that which cannot be named, the name above all names. There are many books and writings of my word. They are all my words. Hear them and feel the emotion that comes from within. Things are not as they may seem. Challenge your beliefs. Open your mind to the enormity of what is before you. There are no limitations. If you can visualize it, it can be. Open your soul, heart, and mind. That is where you will find me and your truth.

—SOURCE

Preface

I am light and love. I come to you with the offering of remembering. You have lived many lifetimes, same as I. I channeled this text from Source to help you remember who you truly are, why you chose this life, and how you can be all that your soul knows you can be.

The truth in these words is profound if you choose to see it. Do not be concerned with the author. The focus is on you. Who are you? Who do you want to be in this lifetime? It is up to you. You are in control.

Glory be to all that is.
Release and remember, your soul is waiting.

-VICTORIA WRIGHT

TABLE OF CONTENTS

Elucidations... 1

Affirmations... 19

Meditations... 29

Elucidations

Welcome

Love, life, wisdom, knowledge, peace, joy,
energy, happiness, laughter, smiles, sunshine.

The wonderous things in life are all around us,
we just have to **see**.

Quiet the mind.

Take time to hear nothing. Feel the air,
the ground, it's warmth, or it's coolness.

Use your other senses. More than your mind and your eyes.

Feel, smell, hear, touch.

Feel the energy run through your body. Feel every sensation.

Feel your heart beat. Listen to your breathing.

These sensations help you to connect to me.

They allow your energy to be on my frequency.

They allow me to talk to you, that which exists in the physical.

The more peaceful or happy you feel,
the more open you are to hearing and feeling me.

I am here to help you create the life you want.

Open and free, happy, and joyful. Where love is all around.

Your truest self is experiencing the wonders of this world
and the amazingness of what is called the physical life.

When a connection is made to me,
life becomes clearer, love becomes deeper.

All of this is waiting for you.

What is love?

Love is energy.

Love is feeling.

Love is bottomless and never ending.

Love is healing.

Love is laughter.

Until you can accept love freely
you will not be able to give love freely.

Everyone desires love, but many are unable to accept it.

Learn to love by loving yourself fully.

This is the purest form of love.

Love is limitless.

Love is what I give to you
unconditionally.

Energy

Energy is the source of all.

Energy is love.

Energy is light.

Energy is hate.

Energy is fear.

Energy is all.

Energy attracts energy.

You have the ability to **decide
what type of energy you will attract**.

Energy is everywhere and everything.

Energy is life.

Energy is the source of all.

Beliefs

Beliefs are what you have been told.

They come from others **who thought they knew.**

Beliefs can be strong and unyielding. Beliefs can mislead.

Beliefs can be shaken.

Why believe when you can **know?**

Release your beliefs.

Let them go.

Start anew and feel.

When the feeling is pure and strong it is knowing.

Knowing is truth – your truth.

Beliefs are someone else's.

Know you and all will be well.

Pain

Emotional pain is the release of old beliefs.

What you thought should be because
of what someone else said.

Pain is the cleansing of another's beliefs
to make room for your own.

Physical pain is the result of holding on to someone else's
beliefs so strongly that it manifests in your body.

It becomes an internal fight.

The knowing you is trying to release,
but the believing you is fighting it.

Only until you truly **let go** of the beliefs you
hold onto and **know you**, will the pain go away.

Release.

Release.

Release.

Knowing

Knowing is that the sun rises and sets.

Knowing is that I am here for you now and always.

Knowing is to follow my word, whatever I may say.

Knowing is that you will never fall.

Knowing is to hear me in the wind, in your heart and in your head.

Knowing is the beating of your heart.

Knowing can be easy but it can also be hard.

Knowing is different than what you **believe**.

Knowing is me, belief is them. I know all.

Knowing is loving me.

Free Will

Free will is a magnificent experience.

It defines who you are.

It is your free will that allows you to experiment with life.

It shows you the options you have before you.

Every time you hear me, you always have
the free will and choice to follow.

There is no right or wrong way.

You have free will for a reason –
to experience life in its fullness.

Following me is like a hawk soaring in the sky
when it catches the wind. It flies effortlessly.

The hawk may flap it wings or glide, but it still flies.
It's the experience that is different.

My will for you is to glide effortlessly in your flight.

Know, I will always provide the wind. I will not let you fall.

What is Time?

Time, as you know it, is an illusion.

What we believe now is already the past, and what we think is future can never be felt because it is already gone.

Time is presence.

Either you are present, or **you are not.**

Time is now and now only, and even then it is fleeting.

Time cannot be managed, kept, gotten ahead of, or delayed.

Time is now and only now. Time is presence.

To Be Present

Presence is knowing that you are breathing.

Presence is feeling your heartbeat.

Presence is feeling the hair on your arms tingle.

Presence is feeling the air, hearing the wind,
and smelling the rain.

Presence is when **your senses are alive.**

All of them.

Presence is beautiful and energizing.

Presence is the only thing we truly have.

Appreciation

Appreciation is the recognition of abundance.

Want is the belief of lack.

Appreciation creates a strong positive energy.

The energy that creates manifestations.

Appreciate what you have every day.

From the love of your life to the most mundane task.

There is always something or someone to appreciate.

There is always someone or something to thank.

You are not alone.

Nothing that is done is solely done by you.

When you appreciate, you give love and joy to others.

Your recognition of their gift is a gift back to them.

Appreciate all the abundance in your life.

You have so much.

Acknowledge it, appreciate it and in return you
will find even more abundance comes to you.

Time is Now

It is time, now more than ever.

People need to hear my words.

You will deliver.

Many will deliver.

I need you to spread my word.

Listen. Hear. The words come from everywhere.

Don't be afraid and don't ever be concerned.

Those that want to hear **will**.

Those who do not **will not**.

You will know when and who to share.

Tell those that are ready to hear the time is now.

Do what you do best.

The message will be heard loud and clear.

Change is happening all around.

The consciousness is awakening.

People are **remembering** who they are and their purpose.

You are one of many throughout this world
that have been chosen to share my word.

Messages may differ but they all are the same.

Love!

Love!

Love!

Affirmations

Uniquely Perfect

I am beautiful.

I am perfect.

Everything about me is perfect in every way.

My light shines from within.

I have the ability to love myself, to love and be loved.

The definition of perfect is how I see it.

It is not what others believe for me
or what I see in the media.

Perfect is me **right now** at this moment.

With all the bumps, lumps, aches,
pains, anxieties, and fears.

I am perfect.

Know that at this exact moment, I am perfect.

No comparisons.

I am me and only I can be me.

I am perfect.

My perfection looks different from someone else.

That is exactly how it should be.

I enjoy me in **all my glory.**

When I feel my own perfection others will see it as well.

I am perfect in all my uniqueness.

I am perfect.

Opportunities Abound

Today is a beautiful day,
filled with new and wonderful opportunities.

My day is what I make it.

I have **unlimited** positive energy
to make my dreams come true.

It is I who determines my opportunity and only I.

Others may help, other may deter but
I have the ability to make opportunities appear.

It is up to me what I do with them.

I have the freedom to choose and know
that more is **always** coming.

I have the energy to make this so.

I believe that, know that, and live that.

Today is a beautiful day, filled
with new and wonderful opportunities.

Purpose

I am one of a kind.

I have a purpose.

My purpose is special to me, but it benefits all of mankind.

I may heal.

I may channel.

I may create.

I may comfort.

I may love.

My purpose is mine, but I share it freely.

Not all will appreciate my purpose, but those that do
will receive an enormous gift.

This gift will help them.

I will not be shy.

I will not be scared.

My purpose is to share my gift, no matter what it is.

The happiness my gift brings to me will
provide happiness to so many others.

In the end all our purpose's is to love.

To love myself and to love others.

This is the greatest gift and the
most important purpose of all.

Power

I am powerful.

My energy is strong when it is focused.

I can move mountains.

I am powerful.

I welcome this power because it is all good.

I use it to heal, to love, to comfort.

I am powerful.

My pure and positive energy is my power.

I use it, share it, refine it.

Everything has energy and everything reacts to energy.

My pure positive energy creates
waves of beauty, love, and joy.

I use it, share it, love it.

I am powerful.

Enlightment

I am connected.

I am knowing.

I am enlightened.

I am enlightened.

I am enlightened.

I am transcending the physical and non-physical.

I am special.

I have been chosen.

I am enlightened.

I am moving through space and time.

I remember the wisdom that
I have gained over many lifetimes.

I am chosen.

I am ready.

I take flight.

I regularly leave this world and travel the universe.

I see, I learn, I teach.

I am light.

I am sun.

I am love.

I am enlightened.

I am peace.

I float, I travel, I see, I feel, I heal.

I am free.

Meditations

You Are Worthy

To begin find a comfortable position and close your eyes.
Take a deep breath in through your nose and out
through your mouth. Breathe in peace and
breathe out any tension that you may have.

As you continue to breathe feel yourself sink comfortably
into the surface you are resting on.

Now in your mind count backwards from 10 to 1.
When you reach one you will be completely relaxed.

[PAUSE]

You are worthy of all your desires.

You are worthy of love.

You are worthy of light.

You are worthy of life.

Every day is a new day and a new beginning.

Every hour, every minute and every second is
the opportunity to be better than the last.

You are worthy of grace and confidence.

You are worthy of trust and forgiveness.

You are worthy of all that you desire.

[REFLECT]

Now imagine a basket of apples.

Beautiful red, green and yellow apples.

Some are shiny and bright, and others are scarred,
dull and bruised. Each of us is like an apple.
We are all different yet the same.

[VISUALIZE]

Our skin or outer self is strong but can be hurt and
bruised. These bruises can lead to rot. The rest of the
apple may be sweet and juicy, but if the rot is allowed
to grow it will take over the entire apple.

Some may think that the rotten apple has no worth, but
everything has value. The apple has the ability to become
a beautiful new tree through its seeds. It takes time, love,
and patience. This new tree then creates many new apples
– each one with the opportunity to be shiny and bright.

[PAUSE]

Every day, minute, and second you have the opportunity
to be better and shine because you are worthy. You are
worthy to have another chance. You are worthy of
self-love. You are worthy to be kind and loving.
You are worthy of light. You are worthy of life.
You are worthy of all your desires.

You are worthy because I have made you so.

[REFLECT]

It will soon be time to bring this journey to an end.

[PAUSE]

Take 3 deep breaths and start bringing your awareness
back to your surroundings. When you are ready, open your
eyes and know that you are worthy.

Heart Center

To begin find a comfortable position and close your eyes.
Take a deep breath in through your nose and out through
your mouth. Breathe in calm and breathe out any tension
that you may have. As you continue to breathe feel yourself
sink comfortably into the surface you are resting on.
Deeper and deeper and deeper.

With each breath you become more and more relaxed.
Release your thoughts and let them float away.
You are safe and all is well.

[PAUSE]

Imagine the people, places, and things in your life
that you love and bring you joy. Your family, friends, pets.
The mountains, beaches, park. A type of food,
or a gift you were given.

Feel the love, feel the joy, feel the beauty.

[REFLECT]

Now, visualize collecting all those people, places,
and things and bring them together as you would
collect snow in the winter to make a snowball.

[VISUALIZE]

Gather them all together, gently patting them into a radiant beautiful sphere. What a magnificent sphere you have created filled with beauty, love, and joy. Admire what you have created. Turn it in your hands. See it from all sides. Appreciate what you have created.

[REFLECT]

Now, gently take that sphere and place it into your heart center. Feel its warmth. Feel all of the beauty, love and joy filling your heart center. Absorb its beauty. Feel its loving energy fill your heart center. Feel its loving embrace. You are honoring yourself with love, beauty, and joy.

[REFLECT]

Know that you can draw upon this love, joy, and beauty anytime you need it. Grace yourself with it, share it, enjoy it.

[REFLECT]

It will soon be time to bring this experience to a close.

[PAUSE]

Take 3 deep full breaths and begin to bring your awareness gently back to your surroundings. When you are ready, open your eyes and bring love, joy, and beauty to your day.

Reflections

If this book was helpful to you, gift it along to someone
who will also benefit from these words. Include your
name below and the name of the person you are
gifting it to, so all that read this book will know
who has been touched by these words.

I _____ gift this book to _____

I _____ gift this book to _____

I _____ gift this book to _____

I _____ gift this book to _____

I _____ gift this book to _____

I _____ gift this book to _____

I _____ gift this book to _____

I _____ gift this book to _____

I _____ gift this book to _____